# WHY WE CELEBRATE DIWALI

WHY WE CELEBRATE

# Diwali

## Everything to Know about Your Favorite Holiday

ANJALI JOSHI

Illustrations by LUMINA DATAMATICS

callisto publishing
an imprint of Sourcebooks

Illustrations by Lumina Datamatics with the following exceptions:
© I_Mak/Shutterstock: cover (banner); © vivijk/Shutterstock (pattern)
Series Designer: Irene Vandervoort
Art Directors: Jane Archer and Lisa Schreiber
Art Producer: Hannah Dickerson
Editor: Annie Choi
Production Designer: Martin Worthington
Production Editor: Jael Fogle
Production Manager: Jose Olivera



Originally published as *Celebrating Diwali: History, Traditions, and Activities – A Holiday Book for Kids* in 2022 in the United States of America by Callisto Kids, an imprint of Callisto Publishing LLC.

Published by Callisto Publishing LLC C/O Sourcebooks LLC
P.O. Box 4410, Naperville, Illinois 60567-4410
(630) 961-3900
callistopublishing.com

Library of Congress Cataloging-in-Publication Data is on file with the publisher.

This product conforms to all applicable CPSC and CPSIA standards.

Source of Production: Wing King Tong Paper Products Co.Ltd. Shenzhen, Guangdong Province, China
Date of Production: November 2024
Run Number: 5044963

Printed and bound in China.
WKT 10 9 8 7 6 5 4 3 2 1

This book is dedicated to all the first- and second-generation immigrant parents who are striving to preserve traditions and culture for the next generation while navigating and understanding their own hyphenated identities.

# CONTENTS

What Is Diwali?
1

History and Folklore
2

Preparing for Diwali
9

How to Celebrate Diwali
15

Around the World
22

Culture Corner
28

Learn to Say It!
36

Glossary
37

Resources
39

# WHAT IS DIWALI?

Diwali is one of the most popular holidays in India. It is the celebration of light over dark, or good over evil. Diwali is also called Deepavali, which means "row of lights." During the festival, people decorate their homes with rows of oil lamps called *diyas*.

Many different people all over the world celebrate this Festival of Lights. The celebration lasts for five days. People share delicious food and sweets with family and friends. Some people wear new clothes and exchange gifts.

The holiday starts in late fall, usually during October or November. The date changes every year because it is based on the Hindu calendar. This **lunisolar calendar** is based on the movements of the moon and the sun.

# HISTORY AND FOLKLORE

Diwali is celebrated by different religions for different reasons. Hindus, Sikhs, Jains, and Newar Buddhists all observe the holiday. There are regional differences in Diwali **traditions** across India. Many families also have their own traditions. Although there are many versions of the holiday, a common theme is the victory of good over evil. It celebrates the forces of light over the forces of dark.

## ANCIENT FESTIVAL

No one knows when exactly Diwali began, but its traditions go back more than 2,500 years! Some say it started as a festival to celebrate the last **harvest** before winter. Back then, many people in India were farmers. During the rainy season, farmers worked hard to grow crops. In fall, they celebrated their harvest and prayed to Lakshmi, the Hindu goddess of wealth and good **fortune**. They hoped she would bless them with a successful year ahead.

Diwali is celebrated on the darkest night of the month, when the moon is not visible in the sky. Some people think that farmers lit diyas outside their houses to attract insects. This would have kept insects away from their crops.

## VICTORY FOR PRINCE RAMA

There are many stories that explain the origin of Diwali. One of them is the Hindu story of Prince Rama. He was a prince in the ancient city of Ayodhya. Prince Rama was **exiled** from the city and forced to live in a forest for fourteen years with his wife, Sita, and his younger brother Lakshman. One day, an evil ten-headed demon named Ravan captured the prince's wife, Sita. He ran away with her to the island of Lanka. Prince Rama was determined to bring Sita back.

Rama's brother Lakshman and their loyal friend Hanuman wanted to help. Hanuman and his army of monkeys built a bridge from India to the island of Lanka to help Rama cross. After a long battle, Prince Rama defeated Ravan and rescued Sita.

When Prince Rama and Sita finally returned to Ayodhya, the streets were lit with millions of beautiful diyas to welcome them home. The city was filled with joyous celebrations for the beloved prince and princess.

# GODS AND GODDESSES

**There are many gods and goddesses in Hinduism. Some gods are avatars, or human forms, of other gods. For example, the god Vishnu has many avatars. Rama and Krishna are both avatars of Vishnu.**

RAMA is the seventh avatar of Vishnu. He is also known as the god of **virtue**. Prince Rama's return home after defeating the demon Ravan is one of the most popular Diwali stories. Like all of Lord Vishnu's avatars, Lord Rama is often shown with blue skin. He holds a bow and arrow.

KRISHNA is the god of protection and love. Some Diwali traditions celebrate Lord Krishna's victory over the evil demon Narakasura. Lord Krishna is also shown with blue skin. He holds a spinning gold disk on one finger, which he uses as a weapon in battles.

GANESH is the god of wisdom and the remover of obstacles. People pray to Lord Ganesh before they start something new. Ganesh is shown with the head of an elephant. He also rides a mouse to get around!

LAKSHMI is the goddess of wealth and good fortune. People believe she visits homes during Diwali. Lakshmi is often shown sitting on a pink lotus flower as her throne. She has four hands with gold coins coming out of them.

## LORD KRISHNA AND NARAKASURA

In some parts of southern India, Diwali celebrates Lord Krishna's victory over Narakasura. In this story, Narakasura was a demon who caused pain and suffering in the world. Lord Krishna was called upon to fight the demon. Although Narakasura used many weapons against Krishna, they were no match for Lord Krishna's fast-spinning disk! When Lord Krishna defeated Narakasura, peace was restored on Earth.

## CELEBRATING LAKSHMI

On the third day of Diwali, Hindu families gather to pray to the goddess Lakshmi. They also pray to Ganesh, who is known as the god of wisdom. People believe that Lakshmi visits homes on the third night of Diwali to bring good fortune. Families clean and decorate their homes to prepare for her visit. They buy or make marigold **garlands** and light diyas to welcome the goddess into their homes. Some traditions celebrate Diwali as the day that Lakshmi was born. She is believed to have been born from the churning of the ocean by gods and demons.

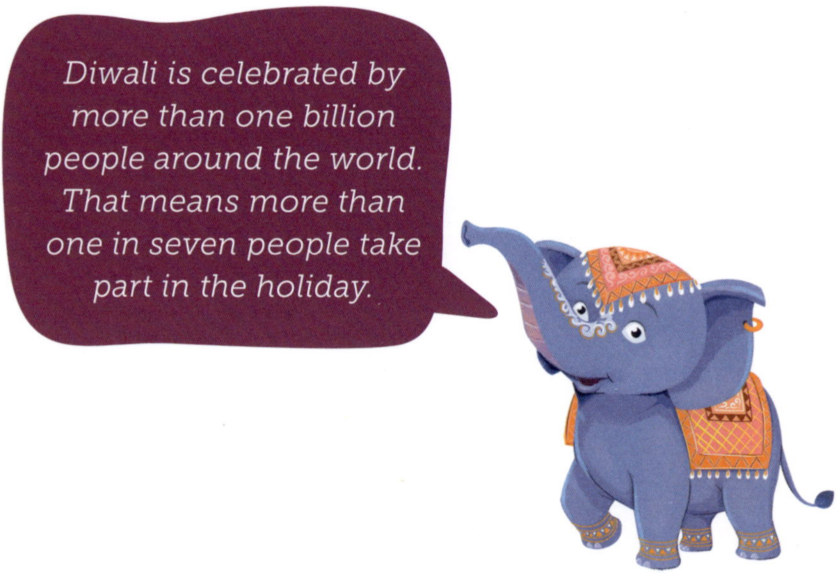

# PREPARING FOR DIWALI

There are many ways to celebrate Diwali. Different parts of India and different religions have their own Diwali traditions. Here are some common ways that people get ready for the festival.

## DECORATE YOUR HOME

Hindus believe that Lakshmi only visits clean homes that are well decorated. That is why tidying the home is an important ritual. One way you can celebrate Diwali is to clean your home and light it up! Traditionally, people use diyas to create festive lighting. You can decorate by putting string lights outside your room or home. Paper lanterns and electric tealights can also be used for the holiday.

## MAKE YOUR OWN RANGOLI

People prepare for Diwali by decorating with flowers, lanterns, and *rangoli*. Rangoli, also known as *kolam*, are beautiful designs made of colorful powdered rice. People pour these powders on the ground in front of their homes, usually in the shape of flowers, diyas, or peacock feathers. (Find out

how to make your own colored rice on page 33.) You can also make vibrant patterns using a variety of other materials, such as pattern blocks, bright-colored construction paper, or even plain white paper and markers! Another way to create patterns outside your home is with sidewalk chalk.

## THROW A DIWALI PARTY

Family and friends gather during Diwali to celebrate together. People plan big parties that include lots of food, music, and dancing. Why not plan your own Diwali party? Start by making invitations and sending them to family and friends. You can decorate your invitations with pictures of fireworks and lights.

Your Diwali party can include playing your favorite games, listening to music, dancing, and enjoying food together.

## MAKE DELICIOUS FOOD

Food is a big part of Diwali celebrations. In some parts of India, like Maharashtra, people cook *faral* for their guests. Faral is a collection of different sweets and snacks. It is shared with friends and family who visit. Most Diwali **feasts** include finger foods like deep-fried snacks, spicy pastries, and sweets. You can celebrate Diwali by preparing your own finger foods, such as chips, mini sandwiches, or mini cupcakes. Try the recipe on page 30 to make your own Indian-inspired sweet treat!

## SPREAD KINDNESS

Diwali is all about spreading light and love. You can spread kindness by doing nice things for your friends, family, or people in your community. Try bringing a treat to a friend, making them a Diwali card, or writing them a letter to show your appreciation. Any small act of kindness can make a difference and light up someone's day!

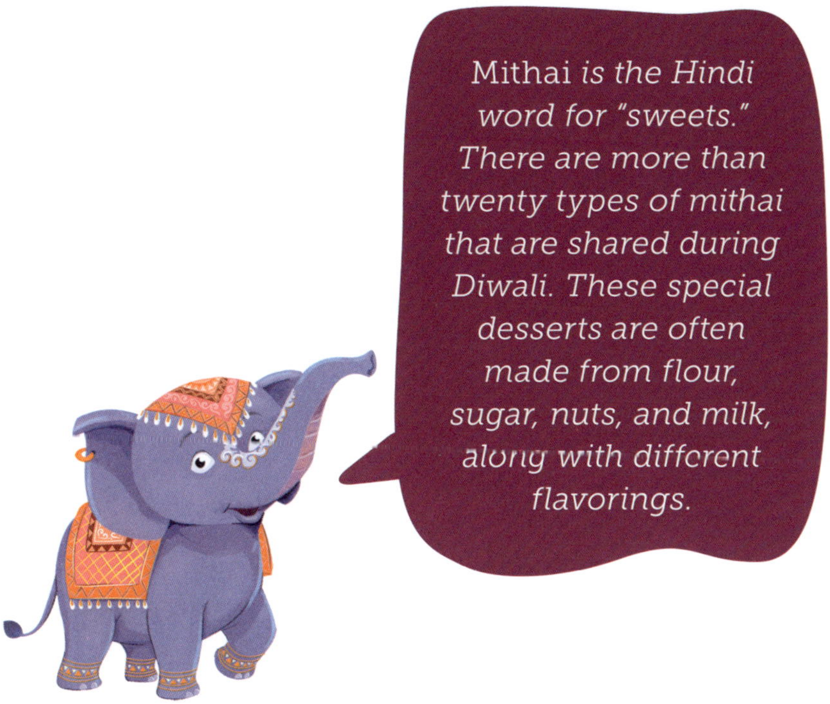

# WHAT TO WEAR

Many people buy new clothes during Diwali to get into the holiday spirit. Traditional Indian clothes for women or girls include *salwar kameez*, *lehengas*, and *saris*. A salwar kameez has pants and a long shirt or tunic. A lehenga has a blouse and a long, flowy skirt. A sari is made of a long piece of fabric that is elegantly tied around the body. These outfits are made with a variety of beautiful fabrics, like chiffon, cotton, and silk. They are often decorated with rhinestones, jewels, and glitter. Traditional Indian clothes for men or boys include *kurtas* and *sherwanis*. A kurta is a light, loose tunic. A sherwani is a more fitted tunic and pants, often made from heavier fabric like brocade. People wear jewelry with their outfits to add even more glamour!

# HOW TO CELEBRATE DIWALI

The festival of Diwali lasts five days. Although there are weeklong celebrations, there are also specific traditions that take place on each day.

## DAY 1

The first day of Diwali is called Dhanteras, which is a celebration of good health and wellness. According to Hindu **legend**, Lord Dhanwantari rose from the sea on this day. He brought Ayurveda, a traditional form of medicine that uses herbs and food to heal the body. Hindus believe that this is an **auspicious** day. They go shopping for gold, silver, and other valuable metals on this day. Dhanteras kicks off the week of celebration!

## DAY 2

The second day of Diwali is called Narak Chaturdashi, but sometimes it's called Choti Diwali, which means "small Diwali." This is because it is the day before the main celebration. People believe that Lord Krishna defeated the evil demon Narakasura on this day. During Narak Chaturdashi, many Hindus take a holy bath to cleanse themselves of evil. They believe that bathing can make the body healthy. Traditionally, people stayed home on this day to prepare for Goddess Lakshmi's arrival. Nowadays, this is typically when families visit one another to exchange gifts and holiday treats.

## DAY 3

The third day of Diwali is when the main celebration takes place. In Hindu legend, this is the day that Lord Rama returned to Ayodhya after defeating the evil demon Ravan. It is also called Lakshmi Pooja because Hindus pray to Lakshmi on this day. On the evening of the third day, many families gather to pray for good fortune and wealth. Sometimes, they also invite a priest to lead them in prayers. People light up their homes with candles, millions of firecrackers are set off, and the streets of India are filled with lights. Family gatherings also take place, which include music, dancing, and feasting on a variety of foods. Traditionally, a prepared meal would be offered to the gods and goddesses after prayers. Then, the family would all enjoy the meal.

*Over the centuries, the name Kali Pooja became more popular than Lakshmi Pooja in Bengal and other eastern parts of India. People in these regions worship Goddess Kali instead of Goddess Lakshmi.*

# LET'S PLAY A GAME!

Diwali is the perfect time to play games. One popular game you can play during Diwali is called Antakshari. In Sanskrit, Antakshari means "last letter." In this musical game, one person begins by singing a verse of a song. The next person continues by singing a verse of a different song. Their song has to begin with the last letter of the previous verse. Music is an important part of Indian culture. Indian cinema has many movies with lots of singing and dancing.

## DAY 4

The fourth day of Diwali is called Vishwakarma. People celebrate this day in many ways. In western India it is known as Bestu Varas, which marks the beginning of the new year. In northern India, they call it Govardhan Pooja. According to Hindu legend, this is the day when Lord Krishna used his strength to lift the Govardhan mountain. This protected the people in the city of Vrindavan during a terrible storm. To celebrate and remember this act of kindness, some Hindus prepare a large **vegetarian** feast to thank Lord Krishna. Many families also give gifts and make **donations** to spread cheer during this special time.

## DAY 5

The fifth and last day of Diwali is a special day for brothers and sisters. It is called Bhai Dooj or Bhai Beej. On this day, brothers visit their sisters. The sisters prepare sweets for their brothers. They also place a dab of holy paste, called *tilak*, on their brothers' foreheads. Tilak is a **symbol** of protection. In return, brothers give gifts to their sisters. Some Hindus believe this tradition began when Lord Krishna defeated the evil demon Narakasura. When he returned home, his sister Subhadra welcomed him with sweets and flowers. Subhadra placed tilak on Krishna's forehead as a symbol of her love. Nowadays, the fifth day of Diwali is a celebration for siblings. They share meals together, enjoy plenty of sweets, and exchange gifts.

# AROUND THE WORLD

Diwali is not just celebrated in India. Millions and millions of people across ninety different countries celebrate Diwali in their own special way. Anyone can join the festivities!

## CELEBRATING IN THE UNITED STATES

Every year, more than six million Americans celebrate Diwali. Across the United States, many local South Asian community groups and local temples organize events and festivities. Much like in India, people gather with friends and family to feast together and exchange gifts. They also light lamps and set off fireworks.

## CELEBRATING IN NEPAL

Diwali is known as Tihar in Nepal. People in Nepal not only pray to gods and goddesses, but they also

**honor** animals. During Diwali, special celebrations take place to worship the crow, the dog, and the cow. Newar Buddhists in Nepal also celebrate Diwali. For them, it marks the day that Emperor Ashoka became a Buddhist. The day is also referred to as Ashok Vijayadashami.

## CELEBRATING IN THE UNITED KINGDOM

The United Kingdom is home to many South Asians. Many cities organize Diwali parties and celebrations. This includes parades, firework shows, and Indian food and music festivals. The biggest Diwali party outside of India takes places in Leicester, England. More than 35,000 people gather to celebrate in this city. The holiday includes the lighting of 6,500 lights on what is known as "The Golden Mile." This celebration takes months to plan and includes plenty of activities, food, music, and dancing.

## CELEBRATING IN SRI LANKA

Diwali is a major celebration in Sri Lanka. Just like in India, people celebrate Diwali by lighting candles and gathering with friends and family. In Sri Lanka, they also make small statues of Hindu gods and goddesses using sugar crystals called *mishri*. People decorate their homes with string lights and diyas, and they also set off firecrackers.

## CELEBRATING IN SINGAPORE

In Singapore, Diwali is a major festival and public holiday. The Little India neighborhood of Singapore celebrates Diwali with lights and decorations. The shops in Little India become very busy with people buying new clothes, jewelry, and flowers. Even grocery stores are busy with shoppers buying ingredients for their favorite Diwali recipes.

# THAT'S DELICIOUS!

*Jalebi* is a popular Indian dessert, especially for kids. Jalebi is made from a flour batter that is deep-fried and then soaked in a sugary syrup. It has a swirly, curly shape. It is crunchy, chewy, sticky, and gooey all at once. This makes it really fun to eat! Although jalebi is enjoyed in every part of India, it is probably not actually Indian. The name comes from the Arabic word *zubaliya*. Some people say it was brought to India from the Middle East thousands of years ago.

# CELEBRATING ACROSS RELIGIONS

Different religions have different Diwali traditions. Sikhs celebrate Bandi Chhor Divas, which translates to "Day of Liberation." This holiday celebrates the day that Guru Hargobind was released from prison. Guru Hargobind was a courageous warrior who fought for people to be treated fairly. Sikhs celebrate the victory of good over evil on this day.

Jains celebrate Diwali in honor of Prince Mahavira. He was a wise prince who traveled all over India to share his wisdom with everyone. On Diwali, Jains light lamps, sing songs, and **meditate** together.

Newar Buddhists celebrate Diwali to mark the day that Emperor Ashoka **abandoned** his violent ways and became a Buddhist. Buddhist families chant and remember the Buddha on Diwali.

*Gold is an important part of Indian culture and traditions. It is such a popular gift that Indian households hold about 11 percent of all the gold in the world!*

# CULTURE CORNER

There are many different crafts and foods you can make for Diwali. Try these activities at home with your family and friends! Remember to always get permission and help from an adult when you do any of the activities.

# SECRET TURMERIC MESSAGE

Turmeric is a bright yellow spice commonly used in Indian cooking. For this activity, you will use turmeric to reveal a top-secret invisible message! Turmeric can stain skin and clothes, so it is best to wear gloves and a smock while doing this activity.

---

**1 tablespoon baking powder**

**½ cup water**

**1 cotton swab**

**White paper**

**1 teaspoon turmeric powder**

**½ cup rubbing alcohol**

**Paintbrush**

1. In a small bowl, mix the baking powder with the water. This will be the "invisible ink."
2. Dip the tip of the cotton swab in the baking powder mixture. Use the tip to write a message on the paper, such as "Happy Diwali!" Let the paper dry completely.
3. In another small bowl, ask an adult to mix the turmeric powder with rubbing alcohol. Never handle rubbing alcohol on your own.
4. Dip the paintbrush in the turmeric solution. Paint over the entire paper to reveal the secret message.

# NO-BAKE CHOCOLATE LADOOS

A *ladoo* is a popular Indian dessert that looks like a donut hole. People often serve ladoos during religious festivities. They can be made from a variety of different flours, including wheat flour or chickpea flour. Traditional ladoos can take hours to make and include clarified butter. This recipe is a quick version that requires no cooking! These ladoos can be enjoyed for up to one week when stored in the refrigerator.

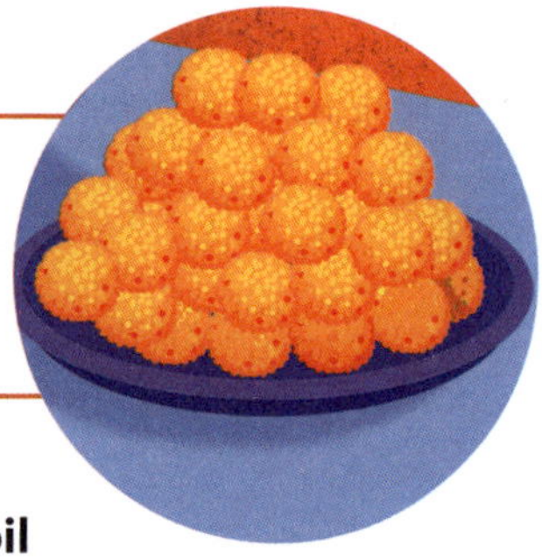

**Yield:** 24 ladoos
**Prep time:** 30 minutes, plus 1 hour to chill

**16 ounces Medjool dates, pitted**

**1⅓ cups old-fashioned rolled oats**

**¾ cup almond flour**

**½ cup unsweetened cocoa**

**¼ cup coconut oil**

**2 tablespoons ground flaxseed**

**¼ cup finely shredded, unsweetened coconut**

1. Line a storage container with parchment paper and set aside.
2. Fill a small bowl with warm water. Soak the dates in the warm water for 20 minutes, then drain the water from the bowl.

3. With the help of an adult, put the dates, oats, almond flour, cocoa, coconut oil, and flaxseed into a food processor. Blend to form a mixture.
4. Remove the mixture from the food processor and place it into a mixing bowl. Using clean hands, form the mixture into balls approximately the size of a golf ball.
5. In a shallow bowl, put the shredded coconut. Roll the ladoo balls in the coconut to coat evenly.
6. Arrange the ladoos in the storage container. Chill in the refrigerator for 1 hour and enjoy.

# CLAY DIYA CANDLE HOLDER

Clay lamps, or diyas, are an important part of Diwali. Why not make your own? In this activity, you'll use air-dry clay to create and decorate diyas!

**Rolling pin**

**Air-dry clay**

**Small bowl, 3-inch to 4-inch diameter**

**Plastic knife**

**Paint**

**Markers**

**Decorating materials like stickers, beads, stick-on jewels, or glitter**

**LED tealight candle**

1. On a clean work surface, use a rolling pin to roll out the clay to an even thickness, about ¼ inch thick.
2. Place the bowl upside down on the rolled-out clay. Use a plastic knife to cut around the bowl. You should have a flat circle.
3. Turn the bowl over. Carefully press the clay circle inside the bowl to create a bowl shape. Leave the clay inside the bowl to dry overnight.
4. When the clay is dry, remove it from the bowl. It's time to decorate your diya!
5. Paint and decorate the diya with anything you like. You can use beads, stickers, or glitter glue.
6. Place the tealight candle in your decorated diya. Turn on your candle. Watch it shimmer and shine as it lights up the room.

# COLORED RICE

Rangoli are made from powdered rice. The colorful rice is arranged in repeating patterns that look like **mandalas**. They can be as detailed as you want! In this activity, you'll make colored rice for your own rangoli designs.

**6 cups uncooked white rice**

**6 sealable plastic storage bags**

**Liquid food coloring in a variety of colors**

**Sidewalk chalk (optional)**

1. Pour 1 cup of rice into each bag.
2. Add 2 teaspoons of food coloring to each bag. Mix food coloring to create new colors as needed. For example, if you only have red and yellow food coloring, combine 1 teaspoon of red and 1 teaspoon of yellow to create orange.
3. Seal the plastic bags. Shake each bag well to coat the rice evenly with food coloring. Repeat for all six bags. You should have six different colors of rice.
4. In a safe space outside, use sidewalk chalk to outline your own rangoli design. If you don't have chalk, you can sketch a design onto a piece of paper for reference.
5. Use the colored rice to fill in your pattern.

# PAPER LEAF GARLAND

In some parts of India, people hang a garland of mango leaves near the entrance of their home. This is called a *toran* or *thoranam*. The garland is considered good luck! In this activity, you'll make your own toran.

---

**A leaf**

**Pencil**

**Construction paper**

**Scissors**

**Markers**

**Hole punch**

**String**

1. Go out for a walk in your neighborhood with an adult. Find a leaf that has an interesting shape.
2. Use a pencil to trace the shape of the leaf on construction paper. Repeat this on different colors of construction paper.
3. Use scissors to cut out the paper leaves. You can use markers to add details to your leaves.
4. With the help of an adult, use a hole punch to make a small hole in each paper leaf.
5. Thread the string through each paper leaf to create a garland.
6. Hang your garland at your doorway or anywhere around your home for good luck!

# PAPER LANTERN

Make your own mini paper lantern that can be used for Diwali decorations! The lantern will look beautiful at night when the light shines through it. Make sure to use an electric tealight candle, not a real candle.

**8 x 11-inch cardstock paper (can be smaller)**

**Ruler**

**Pencil**

**Scissors**

**LED tealight candle**

**Milk bottle lid**

**Clear tape**

**Decorating materials like markers, stickers, and washi tape**

**12-inch strip cardstock paper**

1. Fold the cardstock paper in half, lengthwise.
2. Use a ruler and pencil to draw short lines along the folded edge. The lines should be evenly spaced about 1 inch apart. Do not draw your lines all the way to the opposite edge.
3. Use scissors to cut the lines along the folded edge, making sure not to cut all the way.
4. Place the tealight candle in the milk bottle lid.
5. Unfold the cardstock paper. Wrap the long edge of the paper around the milk bottle lid. Use clear tape to attach the paper to the lid.
6. Secure the top edge of the lantern using clear tape.
7. Cut a 12-inch strip of cardstock to make a handle to the top of your lantern. Use clear tape to attach the handle.
8. Decorate your paper lantern using markers, stickers, washi tape, and other materials.
9. Turn on your candle and watch it light up your celebratory lantern!

# LEARN TO SAY IT!

**Did you know there are 121 different languages spoken in India? Here's how to say "Happy Diwali" in six different ways.**

**Deepavali ki Shubhkamnayein**
दीपावली की शुभकामनाएं
HINDI

**Tihar ko Subhakamana**
तिहारको शुभकामना
NEPALI

**Subho Dipaboli**
শুভ দীপাবলি
BENGALI

**Iniya Deepavali Nalvazhthukkal**
இனிய தீபாவளி நல்வாழ்த்துக்கள்
TAMIL

**Divalichya Subhecha**
दिवाळीच्या शुभेच्छा
MARATHI

**Diwali Mubaraka**
ਦੀਵਾਲੀ ਮੁਬਾਰਕ
PUNJABI

# GLOSSARY

**abandon:** to give up or leave

**auspicious:** bringing success in the future; lucky

**avatar:** the human form of a god or goddess

**donation:** something that is given to a charity, such as money

**exiled:** to be forced to leave one's own country for a long time

**feast:** large meal, typically during a celebration

**fortune:** luck or large amount of money

**garland:** flowers or leaves that are woven together as decoration

**harvest:** all the farm crops that are grown in one season

**honor:** to respect

**legend:** traditional story

**lunisolar calendar:** calendar based on the phases of the moon (moon's orbit around Earth), the movement of the sun (Earth's orbit around the sun), and the seasons

**mandala:** Hindu and Buddhist symbol that is made of repeating lines and shapes

**meditate:** to think deeply and focus the mind, in silence or with chanting

**symbol:** something that stands for something else

**tradition:** custom or belief that has been passed down from one generation to another

**vegetarian:** food that does not use animal meat

**virtue:** behavior or quality in a person that is thought of as good

# RESOURCES

## BOOKS

Heiligman, Deborah. *Holidays Around the World: Celebrate Diwali: With Sweets, Lights, and Fireworks.*

Joshi, Anjali. *Let's Celebrate Diwali.* Illustrated by Tim Palin.

Thapan, Anita Raina. *Hurray for Diwali!*

Umrigar, Thrity. *Binny's Diwali.* Illustrated by Nidhi Chanani.

## WEBSITES

**Dipal's Diwali Video:**

youtube.com/watch?v=9aSkESrxXs4&ab_channel=TwinklKids%27TV

**Globe Trottin' Kids:**

globetrottinkids.com/diwali-festival-of-lights

**Diwali: Festival of Lights:**

kids.nationalgeographic.com/pages/article/diwali

# ABOUT THE AUTHOR

**Anjali Joshi** is a science teacher, curriculum developer, and the author of several children's books, including *ABC Science Book*, *Sarla in the Sky*, and *Little Jagadish and the Great Experiment*. She holds a master's degree in science education from the University of Oxford. Anjali lives in Toronto, Canada, with her husband and two boys.

# ABOUT THE ILLUSTRATOR

With artists in the US, Europe, and India, **Lumina Datamatics** specializes in educational content for learners of all ages. From simple technical art to complex illustrations, Lumina's team of more than forty-five artists offers a range of design and visual storytelling services to bring instructional content to life.